First Facts®

Spotlight on the Continents

SPOTLIGHT ON
AUSTRALIA

by Xavier Niz

CAPSTONE PRESS
a capstone imprint

First Facts is published by Capstone Press,
151 Good Counsel Drive, P.O. Box 669, Mankato, Minnesota 56002.
www.capstonepub.com

 Books published by Capstone Press are manufactured with paper
containing at least 10 percent post-consumer waste.

Library of Congress Cataloging-in-Publication Data
Niz, Xavier.
 Spotlight on Australia / by Xavier Niz.
    p. cm.—(First facts. Spotlight on the continents)
 Includes bibliographical references and index.
 Summary: "An introduction to Australia including climate, landforms, plants, animals,
and people"—Provided by publisher.
 ISBN 978-1-4296-6627-5 (library binding)
 1. Australia--Juvenile literature. 2. Australia—Geography—Juvenile literature. I. Title.
 DU96.N596 2011
 994—dc22   2010037110

Editorial Credits
Lori Shores, editor; Gene Bentdahl, designer; Laura Manthe, production specialist

Photo Credits
Alamy/david hancock, 20; imagebroker, 19; ImageState, 16
Corbis/Royalty Free, 1
DigitalVision, 14 (top right)
Shutterstock/deb22 (top left), 14; Hans Meerbeek, 14 (bottom left); Ian Scott, 14 (bottom
     right); Jaykayl, 9 (bottom); kwest, cover; Maria Skaldina, 13 (top); Martin Horsky,
     12; Neale Cousland, 9 (top); Radim Spitzer, 13 (bottom)

Artistic Effects
Shutterstock/seed

Essential content terms are **bold** and are defined at the bottom of the page
where they first appear.

Printed in the United States of America in Melrose Park, Illinois.
092010   005935LKS11

TABLE OF CONTENTS

CONTINENTS OF THE WORLD

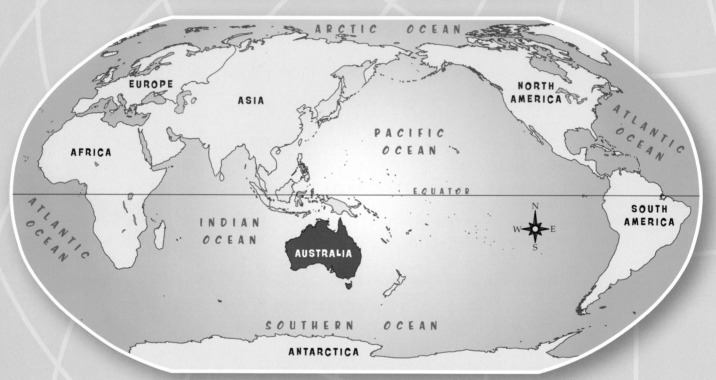

AUSTRALIA

Australia is often called the land down under because it lies below the **equator**. It is the world's smallest **continent**. Australia covers about 3 million square miles (7.8 million square kilometers). It is just a little smaller than the United States. But Australia is the largest island in a group of islands called Oceania.

equator—an imaginary line around the middle of Earth
continent—one of Earth's seven large landmasses

FAST FACTS ABOUT
AUSTRALIA

- 🌐 **Population:** 21,515,754

- 🌐 **Number of independent nations:** 1

- 🌐 **Largest cities:** Sydney, Melbourne, Brisbane, Perth, Adelaide

- 🌐 **Longest river:** Darling, 1,702 miles (2,739 kilometers)

- 🌐 **Highest point:** Mount Kosciusko, 7,310 feet (2,228 meters) above sea level

- 🌐 **Lowest point:** Lake Eyre, 49 feet (15 meters) below sea level

STATES AND TERRITORIES OF AUSTRALIA

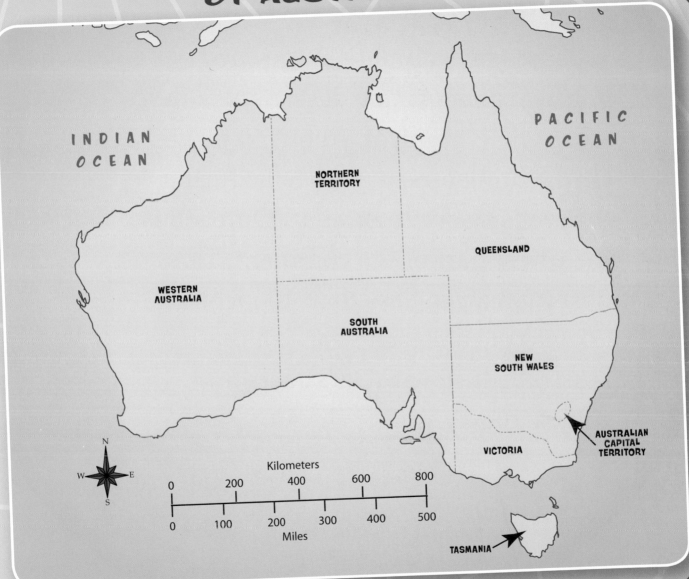

INDIAN OCEAN

PACIFIC OCEAN

NORTHERN TERRITORY

QUEENSLAND

WESTERN AUSTRALIA

SOUTH AUSTRALIA

NEW SOUTH WALES

VICTORIA

AUSTRALIAN CAPITAL TERRITORY

TASMANIA

Kilometers
0   200   400   600   800

Miles
0   100   200   300   400   500

CLIMATE

Australia's **climate** ranges from hot, wet areas to dry deserts. Northern Australia is **tropical**. About 60 inches (152 centimeters) of rain falls during the wet season. Australia's Outback is the driest part of the continent. This desert area gets less than 10 inches (25 cm) of rain each year. Southern Australia has warm summers and cold winters.

climate—the usual weather that occurs in a place
tropical—warm and wet

LANDFORMS OF AUSTRALIA

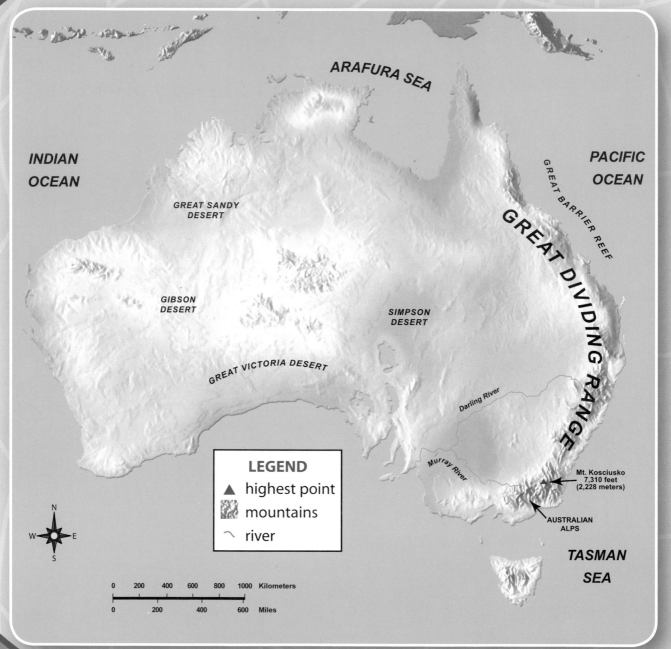

INDIAN OCEAN

ARAFURA SEA

PACIFIC OCEAN

GREAT SANDY DESERT

GREAT BARRIER REEF

GREAT DIVIDING RANGE

GIBSON DESERT

SIMPSON DESERT

GREAT VICTORIA DESERT

Darling River

Murray River

Mt. Kosciusko
7,310 feet
(2,228 meters)

AUSTRALIAN ALPS

TASMAN SEA

LEGEND
▲ highest point
▨ mountains
⌒ river

N
W E
S

| 0 | 200 | 400 | 600 | 800 | 1000 | Kilometers |

| 0 | 200 | 400 | 600 | Miles |

LANDFORMS

The Great Dividing Range towers over Australia's flat land. The Darling river flows from these mountains. It joins the Murray river, which begins in the Australian Alps.

Little water flows in the deserts that cover western Australia. The Great Sandy, Gibson, and Great Victoria Deserts are found there.

PLANTS

Trees grow all over Australia.
In wet areas, eucalyptus trees grow tall.
These trees are short in dry areas.
Palm and fig trees grow along
Australia's wet north coast. Tree ferns
grow on the rainy east coast.

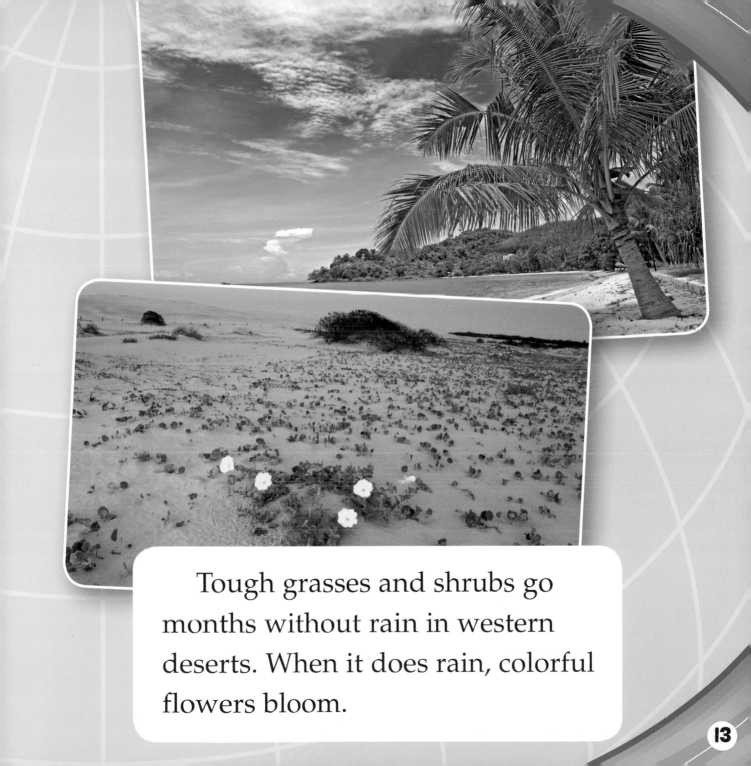

Tough grasses and shrubs go months without rain in western deserts. When it does rain, colorful flowers bloom.

ANIMALS

Australia is home to many unique animals. Australia's emus don't fly, but these large birds run fast. Kangaroos hop across deserts, while koalas sleep in eucalyptus trees. These **marsupials** live only in Australia.

The Great Barrier **Reef** off the east coast of Australia is home to many sea creatures. Here colorful rabbit fish swim past giant clams.

marsupial—an animal that carries its young in a pouch
reef—a strip of rock, coral, or sand near the surface of the ocean

POPULATION DENSITY OF AUSTRALIA

INDIAN OCEAN

PACIFIC OCEAN

N
W · E
S

AUSTRALIA

People per square mile		People per square kilometer
Less than 2		Less than 1
2 to 25		1 to 10
25 to 125		10 to 50
125 to 250		50 to 100
More than 250		More than 100

SOUTHERN OCEAN

PEOPLE

Other than Antarctica, Australia is the least populated continent. Only about 20 million people live there.

Aborigines were Australia's first people. Europeans began moving to Australia in the 1700s. Australians speak English, although some people still speak **native** languages.

native—having to do with original people who lived in an area

LIVING IN AUSTRALIA

Most Australians live in apartments or houses. Many houses include outdoor areas for barbecues.

Many people in Australia live in cities near the coast. Sydney is Australia's largest city. Other people farm along the Murray River.

AUSTRALIA AND THE WORLD

Around the world, people wear jewelry and use metal made from Australia's minerals. Many of the world's opals and diamonds come from Australia. Bauxite from Australia is used to make aluminum.

Australians' skill at water sports is known worldwide. Australia has some of the world's best surfers, swimmers, and sailors.

GLOSSARY

climate (KLY-muht)—the usual weather that occurs in a place

continent (KAHN-tuh-nuhnt)—one of Earth's seven large land masses

equator (i-KWAY-tuhr)—an imaginary line around the middle of Earth; areas near the equator are usually warm and wet

marsupial (mar-SOO-pee-uhl)—an animal that carries its young in a pouch

native (NAY-tiv)—having to do with original people who lived in an area

reef (REEF)—an underwater strip of rocks, coral, or sand near the surface of the ocean

tropical (TROP-uh-kuhl)—warm and wet

READ MORE

Foster, Karen. *Atlas of Australia.* World Atlases. Minneapolis: Picture Window Books, 2008.

Kalman, Bobbie, and Rebecca Sjonger. *Explore Australia and Oceania.* Explore the Continents. New York: Crabtree Pub. Co., 2007.

Porter, Annaliese. *The Outback.* Broome, Wash.: Magabala Books, 2008.

INTERNET SITES

FactHound offers a safe, fun way to find Internet sites related to this book. All of the sites on FactHound have been researched by our staff.

Here's all you do:

Visit *www.facthound.com*

Type in this code: 9781429666275

Super-cool stuff! Check out projects, games and lots more at **www.capstonekids.com**

INDEX